THE ADULT LEARNER
Strategies for Success

Robert L. Steinbach

A FIFTY-MINUTE™ SERIES BOOK

CRISP PUBLICATIONS, INC.
Menlo Park, California

THE ADULT LEARNER
Strategies for Success

Robert L. Steinbach

CREDITS:
Editor: **Kay Kepler**
Designer: **Carol Harris**
Typesetting: **ExecuStaff**
Cover Design: **Carol Harris**
Artwork: **Ralph Mapson**

Copyright © 1993 Crisp Publications, Inc.
Printed in the United States of America by Bawden Printing Company.

English language Crisp books are distributed worldwide. Our major international distributors include:

CANADA: Reid Publishing Ltd., Box 69559—109 Thomas St., Oakville, Ontario, Canada L6J 7R4. TEL: (905) 842-4428, FAX: (905) 842-9327

Raincoast Books Distribution Ltd., 112 East 3rd Avenue, Vancouver, British Columbia, Canada V5T 1C8. TEL: (604) 873-6581, FAX: (604) 874-2711

AUSTRALIA: Career Builders, P.O. Box 1051, Springwood, Brisbane, Queensland, Australia 4127. TEL: 841-1061, FAX: 841-1580

NEW ZEALAND: Career Builders, P.O. Box 571, Manurewa, Auckland, New Zealand. TEL: 266-5276, FAX: 266-4152

JAPAN: Phoenix Associates Co., Mizuho Bldg. 2-12-2, Kami Osaki, Shinagawa-Ku, Tokyo 141, Japan. TEL: 3-443-7231, FAX: 3-443-7640

Selected Crisp titles are also available in other languages. Contact International Rights Manager Suzanne Kelly at (415) 323-6100 for more information.

Library of Congress Catalog Card Number 92-054363
Steinbach, Robert L.
The Adult Learner
ISBN 1-56052-175-9

This book is printed on recyclable paper with soy ink.

PREFACE

The world has changed. It is no longer possible to land a good-paying job after high school and 30 or 40 years later retire from that same job. Even those lucky few individuals who will stay with the same company and in the same job for most of their work life will see the job itself change as computers and other technology permeate the workplace. Demands for increased quality and tougher competition will force all of us to continually upgrade our skills. To be successful in these turbulent times, companies and employees will be constantly pushed to learn, improve and adapt.

The demands of new technology, world-wide competition and the drastic restructuring of giant corporations have shaken our belief in job security. The only real security individuals and companies now have is based on what they know and what they can learn. The future belongs to the learner.

> *"In times of change, learners inherit the earth, while the learned find themselves beautifully equipped to deal with a world that no longer exists."*
>
> —Eric Hoffer

ABOUT THIS BOOK

The Adult Learner examines some of the basic components of effective learning. You will discover your personal learning style. You will explore how new information gets to the brain and how you can maximize that process. You will learn how to listen better, ask the right questions and commit information to memory when necessary. You will apply new and effective methods for old-fashioned skills such as taking useful notes and organizing information.

Other topics include the new learning technologies that are available to you at home, work, school and the public library. You also will learn how to increase comprehension and improve concentration through learner-centered reading and by controlling your external and internal environments. Before we are through, you will find out how to examine and overcome learning fears such as test anxiety, fear of math and negative self-fulfilling prophecies (''I'll never remember all of this.'').

When you finish this book, you will have the tools that you need to continue on your journey as a more effective lifelong learner. The skills and attitudes that you have gained will make you more valuable to yourself and to others. Good luck and good learning!

ABOUT THE AUTHOR

Bob Steinbach is the president of Skill Development Consultants (SDC), an international training and consulting group. SDC seminars have trained more than 4,000 workers and managers of General Motors, Saturn Corp., and Subaru-Isuzu America. Steinbach taught success strategies to adult students at both the university and community college level before forming his own company. He received his B.A. and M.A. from Bowling Green State University in Bowling Green, Ohio.

For information concerning workshops based on this book, contact:

Skill Development Consultants
3477 Lawson Drive
Dayton, OH   45432
(513) 426–6776

CONTENTS

CONTENTS (continued)

INTRODUCTION

Humans are wonderfully designed to be able to learn from the moment of birth. Learning can and should be a lifelong process, not what happens for a short period of time at the beginning of life in a place called school. There have always been people who were true "lifelong learners." These people sought out the opportunity to master new skills, meet new challenges and gain new knowledge. They used that marvelous learning machine (their brain) continually to improve themselves, becoming more valuable to themselves, their employers and society.

The ability to be a lifelong learner is both a competitive advantage and an economic survival requirement. In this book, we will explore how to be as effective as possible at seeking out and meeting the learning opportunities that are all around us. We will focus on the skills that enable us to cope with the demands of training, on-the-job learning and formal schooling, and that make lifelong learning a more enjoyable, rewarding activity.

Some people will need to shift their attitude about why we are caught up in the "learning society." We shouldn't think we learn for somebody else: parents, teachers, coaches and bosses. Even though the company may require training, we must see our time and effort as an investment in ourselves and our futures. Not only should we learn when we "must," we should seek out the opportunity. The future belongs to the companies and people who can keep up with the changes around them.

One last thought on why lifelong learning should be your personal goal: Your life will be better and more interesting for the effort. The old adage "use it or lose it" applies to mental as well as physical well-being. Lifelong learners are sharper, more interesting and more alive. Learning doesn't have to be a chore—it should be an adventure.

USING THE CASE STUDIES

Five fictional case studies have been included to encourage you to think through some of the issues, attitudes and barriers that are part of the lifelong learning process. Since lifelong learners vary so greatly in attitudes, abilities, goals and backgrounds, it is not possible to create examples that fit every situation. The case studies were created from the author's experience and drawn from the backgrounds of many real people; however, no character represents a particular real person.

When reading a case study, put yourself in the position of a trusted friend advising the character. What would you recommend? Compare your thoughts to the author's advice. Look for similarities between the characters' experiences and your own. Have you faced similar problems? Do you share similar skills, abilities and goals? How would you describe yourself in a short case study? Think about that question, because that will be the final activity in the book.

Ronald: A Case Study

Ronald has worked for the same large manufacturing company for 22 years. At age 42, he has a family, house, two cars and a boat. He hopes to retire in his early 50s and enjoy the company's retirement benefits and health plan. In the last few years, however, his company has been shaken by stiff foreign competition and declining sales. Although he has been safe from layoff so far, there are always rumors.

The company has been struggling to regain stability and win back customers. Part of this effort has been to offer training in teamwork, total quality management (TQM) and statistical process control (SPC). Ronald questions the company's motives and has not taken part in training programs. He is busy enough with his own job and family and prefers to be left alone to do his work as he has in the past. Besides, it has been nearly 25 years since he was in school and he didn't care much for it then. From what he knows about SPC and TQM, they both involve math, one of his least favorite subjects.

Why should Ronald bother with school at this stage of his life?

Advice to Ronald

Tens of thousands of American workers could identify with Ronald's situation. Many employees of large companies who felt they had very stable jobs when they were hired are now worried about layoffs, shutdowns and transfers.

Ronald should get involved in one of the training programs around the plant. Companies and unions have realized that the only way American industry can keep its leadership position in the world is to invest heavily in people. Training programs are a way of doing that. The thing that is wrong with continuing to operate as we did in the past is that thousands of good American jobs have been lost doing it the old way. We cannot compete for jobs on cost of labor. There are millions of people who will do it cheaper. We have to compete on skill and knowledge.

There are three reasons to upgrade your skills. The first is to benefit the company by becoming a more valuable employee. Remember those retirement benefits Ronald is counting on? Healthy companies can afford to pay healthy benefits, sick ones can't.

The second reason is to protect yourself. Whatever you learn makes you more valuable. Many people who had stable jobs found themselves looking for work. I hope that never happens to Ronald. However, if it does, knowing about SPC might make the difference between his getting a skilled job or flipping burgers.

Finally, Ronald mentioned retiring in his early 50s. If he lives to the average life expectancy, he would be around at least another 25 years after retirement. Statistics say that most people who retire at that age take another job of some kind or start their own business. Whatever he learns now will benefit him then.

P A R T

1

The ASK Attitude

THE ASK ATTITUDE

Many people actively seek knowledge. Children are quick learners, who absorb information without teachers. This approach is called the ASK (Actively Seek Knowledge) attitude. Learning works best when you seek it without waiting to be forced or coaxed. Young children, especially before the age of five, are active learners. As any parent will tell you, they are into everything: exploring, taking apart, trying, succeeding and failing. ''Why?'' is their burning question. They don't wait for someone to teach them.

That is why so much of the truly important and difficult learning that people do happens so early in life. Children learn challenging skills like how to walk and speak a language with very little formal instruction. They learn without being self-conscious and without fear of failure. They learn without the prodding of teachers and without the threat of a test.

Unfortunately, most schools put the learner in the back seat for most of the school day over 12 long years. Students become reactive. We wait for the teacher to tell us what, when and how to learn. Much of the joy of learning disappears during the process. Look in the window at a kindergarten class and watch the energy and movement. Listen to the excited questions. Then check out a classroom full of adults. In most cases, adults have been trained to wait silently for instructions. They react to the teacher. They worry about grades, stifle questions and fear looking stupid. Often they stare blankly ahead and glance at their watches.

But that childlike learner is still around sometimes. When people pursue a favorite hobby, most tear into it with pleasure. They read everything they can find on the subject, practice new techniques and ask questions. They try and fail and try again. That is active learning; that is the key to successful life-long learning.

SELF-PERCEPTION

By the time we are adults most of us have formed some strong opinions about ourselves. Some of these opinions put us in a positive light: ''I'm a good parent,'' ''I can be trusted.'' Other opinions can limit and stifle us: ''I'm terrible at math,'' ''I'm just not creative,'' ''I'm too uncoordinated for that.''

While knowing and accepting our strengths and weaknesses can be an asset, watch out for negative self-fulfilling prophecies. Many students in math class who thought ''I'm terrible at math'' as they entered the classroom door proved themselves right by shutting down mentally at the first challenge presented to them. Frequently, if they do fail, the real reason is that they were not prepared for *this level* of math. Many times we are not patient enough to start at the level of an activity that we are ready for and build up to where we want to be. Instead, we expect to compete against golfers who have been playing for years, rebuild a motorcycle engine on the first try or be able to make music on a guitar after a lesson or two.

Self-perception alone does not decide the outcome of a challenge. It may be true that it takes one person longer to learn a skill than someone else, and some things may never be mastered, but, for many skills and most types of knowledge, the real difference between success and failure is time and effort, not inborn ability.

> ''*The will to win is nothing without the will to prepare.*''
> —Recent ad for an athletic shoe

TEXTBOOK PREVIEW: AN ACTIVITY

Before reading any further, explore the rest of this book. Skim through looking at headings, illustrations and activities. Read the Table of Contents. When you see something interesting, stop and read a paragraph or two, then record the idea in the space below. Find six ideas that you want to learn more about.

IDEA	PAGE NO.
1.	
2.	
3.	
4.	
5.	
6.	

Congratulations. You have just completed a textbook survey. This simple little task has provided your brain with a road map and some destinations along this learning journey. You have helped yourself get ready to learn by creating a partial image of the content of this book. Your brain naturally seeks to complete partial pictures; a textbook survey helps focus your mind on completing the picture. You should always survey textbooks, manuals and factual articles in magazines as a simple, effective way to increase comprehension and retention.

WARNING: If you did not complete the survey of the book or did not write down six things that you want to learn about, you may be stuck in a reactive learning mode. Remember, you are not learning this material for anyone but yourself. The activities in this book are an essential part of the learning process. Just reading this book is not enough.

ACTIVELY SEEK KNOWLEDGE (ASK)

ASK means Actively Seek Knowledge. If you don't know, ASK. If you are confused ASK. If you can't find it, ASK. If you need help, ASK. If you are curious, ASK.

Lifelong learning is both an attitude and a skill. A lifelong learner tries to look at each new situation or challenge as an opportunity for growth. Remember the example of the children who always ask questions? They have the right idea. People learn by asking questions and finding the answers. It is frightening to see how much energy and curiosity appears to be lost as we age. Many adults pass through their days ignoring the new, the different, the challenging. Some hold on tightly to what they know and avoid learning about new things, new methods and new tools.

Somehow, many people have gotten the mistaken idea that questions, curiosity and mistakes are signs of ignorance. They don't want to admit that they don't know something. In reality, questions are signs that the mind is still alive and that life is still interesting. All too many times the classroom instructor asks, "Are there any questions?," only to be answered with silence and blank stares. Does silence mean understanding? If so, why are so many frustrated hours spent trying to do math homework, make the computer work or follow the new office procedure? If you are in a class and don't understand something, ASK. I'll bet at least five other people missed the same point. You'll never know unless you ASK.

PART

2

Individual Learning Styles

SELF-QUIZ: WHAT'S MY "LEARNING STYLE"?

Check *yes* or *no* beside each of the following statements to reflect how you learn as a general rule. Be honest and think in terms of most of the time, not exceptions.

	YES	NO
1. I learn a lot from listening to instructors and other knowledgeable people.	_____	_____
2. I figure things out best by trial and error.	_____	_____
3. Books are easy for me to learn from.	_____	_____
4. Give me a map and I can find my way.	_____	_____
5. I like to have directions explained to me verbally.	_____	_____
6. I can often assemble something I just bought without looking at the instructions.	_____	_____
7. I learn a lot from discussions.	_____	_____
8. I'd rather watch an expert first and then try a new skill.	_____	_____
9. The best way for me to learn how something works is to take it apart and put it back together.	_____	_____
10. I can remember most of what is said in classes and meetings without taking notes.	_____	_____
11. The classes that I was best at in school involved physical activity and movement.	_____	_____
12. Diagrams and drawings help me understand new concepts.	_____	_____

SELF-QUIZ RESULTS

While it is not a scientific assessment, the self-quiz on page 13 tells you something about how you learn best.

A "yes" to questions 1, 5, 7 and 10 indicates that you learn by hearing it first: you are a "good listener" or strong auditory learner.

A "yes" to questions 3, 4, 8 and 12 indicates that you learn by reading, watching and studying diagrams: you are a strong visual learner.

A "yes" to questions 2, 6, 9 and 11 indicates that you learn by doing things: you are a strong kinesthetic learner.

It is very possible to have strong scores in more than one learning style.

While a short quiz like this cannot diagnose accurately how you learn, it can provide insights into how you see yourself and the learning process. This is especially helpful in understanding how you match up with a particular learning task or instructor. For example, if you are strong kinesthetic learner, you may be frustrated with lectures where you are expected to sit and listen. Becoming a truly effective lifelong learner means maximizing your strengths and minimizing your weaknesses.

> *Each mind has its own method.*
> —Ralph Waldo Emerson

V, A OR K: WHICH ARE YOU?

Visual, auditory and kinesthetic: These three learning modes are the most important ways to move information to the human brain. From very early in life, individuals tend to favor one or two of these modes over the others. Some children understand language at a very early age (auditory), others show a great interest in color and pictures (visual) and still others walk early and quickly learn to throw a ball or play with blocks (kinesthetic).

These natural preferences are seen as talents in the first few years of life, and childhood usually provides plenty of outlets for each learning style. When we start school, however, we find that we can't spend all our time at what we are good at or what we enjoy. While the early grades still provide outlets for physical and artistic learning, traditional high schools concentrate heavily on auditory (sit and listen) and visual learning (be quiet and read).

Many people who were confident and curious as young children lose interest in learning because it seems boring. The truth is that learning itself is rarely boring, but the methods to which teachers and students limit themselves frequently are. To make learning exciting again, it is important to bring the excitement and variety that we enjoyed as children back into the process.

Ann: A Case Study

Ann has always been a very energetic, athletic person. She loves to work with her hands, and her hobbies are artistic and athletic. In high school, she had little interest in college prep classes but excelled in shop, physical education and art. She took a job at age 18 as an assembler in a small job-shop putting together specialized electronic components. She quickly mastered more complicated soldering and assembly tasks and built a reputation as one of the fastest and most dependable workers in the plant.

At age 28, Ann still likes the company but wants to move up into a better-paying supervisory position. She realizes that this will require more education and has begun taking an evening class at the community college. Unfortunately, she finds the lecture format and reading assignments involved in her first class boring and time-consuming. She constantly finds excuses to work around the house or yard in order to avoid settling down to study. She also is finding that she lacks some of the basic writing and study skills that she missed by avoiding college prep classes in high school.

What kind of learner do you think Ann is? What advice would you give her?

CASE STUDY (continued)

Advice to Ann

Ann is a kinesthetic learner: a natural doer, not well designed for the sitting and listening involved in so many formal educational situations. She needs to think about her motives for going to school and seeking a promotion. If the only reason that she wants to move into management is to earn more money, she may want to explore other options. Many industries lack skilled technicians and tradespeople. She may want to pursue training in specialty soldering or welding, or she may want to apply to an apprenticeship program. Ann may also simply let her boss know that she wants a chance to make more money and is willing to take on more challenging tasks.

If, however, she decides that supervision is the route that she wants to take, she must face the fact that colleges are primarily designed for auditory and visual learners and that she will have to upgrade her writing and study habits. The sooner she builds those skills, the less likely deficits in these areas will get in her way. Next, she should accept her kinesthetic nature and try to build it into her approach to education. Ann should do her best to picture herself applying the content of lectures and readings. Creating a vivid image of an activity or situation as she learns about it will make coursework feel more real and appeal to her need for active learning.

Ann should build activity into her learning routine. She should use her artistic and mechanical ability to turn words into diagrams and pictures in her notetaking. When break time rolls around, she should get up and take a quick walk while reviewing the high points of the previous hour. At home, she should study in short bursts punctuated by even shorter bursts of physical activity. While she will need to sit still to read, she can move around while reviewing for tests. A child's chalkboard or dry-erase board could be a useful tool for standup review, diagramming and practice. For kinesthetic learners like Ann, writing, drawing, speaking and moving should be natural parts of the study routine.

A LEARNER'S AUTOBIOGRAPHY: YOUR STORY

One of the best ways to discover your own personal learning style is to analyze successful learning experiences from the past. Complete the following learner's autobiography and look for patterns that can point to your preferred learning style.

1. Describe a learning experience that you feel good about. It can be in or out of school, job- or hobby-related, recent or from many years ago.

   _____

   _____

2. What was your motivation for the learning?

   _____

   _____

3. Where did most of the learning take place?

   _____

   _____

4. How old were you at the time you started the learning?

   _____

   _____

5. What methods did you use to learn?

   _____

   _____

6. What were your feelings during the learning process?

   _____

   _____

7. How much time did you devote to the learning process?

   _____

   _____

8. Who helped you with your learning? How did they help?

   _____

   _____

THINKING ABOUT YOUR LEARNER'S AUTOBIOGRAPHY

Most people can identify a pattern in their successful learning experiences. Look over your answers and try to determine yours. Do you work best alone or in a class? Are you primarily a visual, auditory or kinesthetic learner, or do you utilize all three modes equally? What motivates you? What time of day and what type of learning location seem to help you do your best work?

You may also gain further information from thinking back on a failed learning project. Can you identify the cause of the failure? Was the project too difficult? Did you fail to take an active role in your own learning? Were you reluctant to ask for help when you needed it? Was your motivation for the learning unclear? Did you talk yourself into failing with negative thoughts about your own abilities?

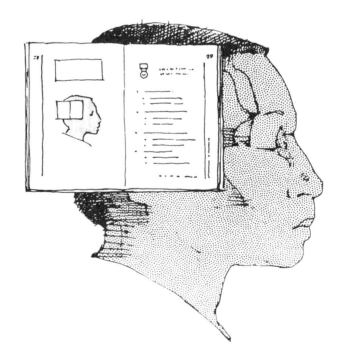

MULTITRACKING: USING ALL THE PATHWAYS

Adults can't expect to enjoy all aspects of learning. Schools can't be expected to make learning to write a decent sentence as much fun as learning to ski. But education can be more effective and more interesting if it involves as many learning modes as possible. An old proverb about learning goes: *Tell me and I will soon forget, show me and I may remember, let me try and I will understand.*

Multitracking means to use all the learning modes when you master new information or skills. The brain remembers by being physically stimulated through the senses. The ears, the eyes and the movement of the body all send different signals. By combining these signals, we leave a more permanent impression on the brain.

Many people mistake being exposed to material with trying to learn it. You must push yourself to become as actively involved with the new learning as possible:

• *While listening to lectures,* examine any visual aids. Take notes and draw diagrams of what you hear. Ask questions and join in discussions. Volunteer to participate in demonstrations or activities. Work the problems along with the math instructor. Use color in your notes to emphasize important points. Recite key points from the class to yourself on the way home. Try anything that will turn a passive ''sit and listen'' situation into a multitrack learning experience.

• *While reading textbooks and manuals,* highlight important information. Make notes in the margin. Read especially difficult material out loud to yourself. Draw diagrams of the new information. Get up and move around as you read. Write out important points in your notebook. If you can try the information now, do it; this is especially effective when reading a manual for a computer or tool—read and do, do and read. Explain what you have read to anyone who will listen. If possible, teach someone else the new skill.

• *While learning a new job or task,* watch carefully. Ask questions. Ask to try the task yourself. Picture yourself performing the new task perfectly. Ask an expert to observe and critique you. Dig in and try; mistakes are part of learning. If mistakes would be too costly, imitate the process in some less risky way. Practice. Then practice some more.

THINKING-STYLE INVENTORY

For each of the items below, put a checkmark next to the choice that is most like you. Check only one choice for each item.

1. When I listen to a song, I pay most attention to the

   _____ words   _____ music

2. I act on hunches

   _____ seldom   _____ often

3. I am best at

   _____ word games   _____ physical games

4. After a movie I'm most likely to remember

   _____ individual scenes   _____ the plot

5. I like to have my job

   _____ carefully planned   _____ flexible

6. My closets and shelves are

   _____ well organized   _____ cluttered

7. I would rather get directions

   _____ out loud   _____ from a map

8. When putting together something new, I

   _____ read directions first   _____ figure it out myself

9. I enjoy activities most that are

   _____ mental   _____ physical

10. I dream

    _____ seldom   _____ often

11. I like to work on projects

_____ one by one   _____ several at a time

12. I am better at

_____ spelling   _____ art

13. I daydream

_____ seldom   _____ often

14. I try new things

_____ seldom   _____ often

15. I prefer to learn by

_____ listening   _____ doing

16. I would rather

_____ explain directions   _____ draw a map

17. Math is something I

_____ enjoy   _____ dislike

18. I pay most attention to

_____ what people say   _____ how they say it

19. My sense of direction is

_____ poor   _____ good

20. I lose track of time

_____ seldom   _____ often

RESULTS OF THE THINKING-STYLE INVENTORY

To score your thinking-style inventory, count the number of check marks in each column. The answers in the left column indicate a more sequential, or "left-brain" thinking style (logical, straight-line, linguistic). The answers in the right column indicate a more creative, open-ended, or "right brain" thinking style (visual, less structured, artistic).

Two Modes of Knowing:

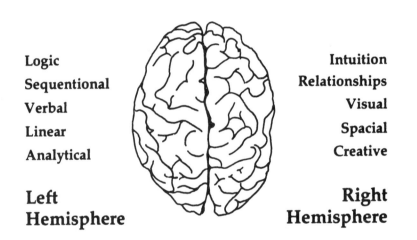

Logic
Sequentional
Verbal
Linear
Analytical

Left Hemisphere

Intuition
Relationships
Visual
Spacial
Creative

Right Hemisphere

Many people overuse one thinking style and underuse the other. Some situations call for a very logical, sequential thinking style; others call for a more creative, open style. It is a great advantage to lifelong learners if they can identify when a particular style is appropriate and use tools and techniques that fit the situation.

Understanding Your Thinking-Style Inventory

The higher the number in a column, the stronger your preference for that thinking style. This is a very short inventory and the results are not conclusive. However, if there is a difference of more than five between your column totals, you may depend heavily on one style of thinking. The following pages contain suggestions for modifying your style according to the situation.

If you need to be more logical and sequential, try:

► *Outlining.* It may seem old-fashioned, but it is a great way to organize information.

► *Prioritizing.* Decide what is most important, which things should be done first and what is the most logical sequence to follow.

► *Using a schedule book or calendar to keep track of time.* If you see yourself as a free spirit, others can see you as unreliable. Organize your time.

► *Making lists.* Lists of things to do can capture your good ideas and make sure they turn into reality.

► *Starting projects early and finishing well before the deadline.* Some people consistently underestimate how much time it will take to finish a paper or project and are always rushing to beat the clock. This decreases the likelihood that they will do their best work and increases their chances of making mistakes.

► *Organizing your work space.* It is very difficult to study or work if you can't find the things you need to do the job.

► *Setting goals with specific deadlines and establishing checkpoints.* This ensures you are progressing at the right pace.

RESULTS OF THE THINKING-STYLE INVENTORY (continued)

If you need to be more creative and open try:

▶ *Brainstorming.* By yourself or with a group, come up with as many ideas as possible to solve a problem or approach a task. Don't judge any of the ideas at first, just write them all down. Later you can sort them out.

▶ *Drawing a mind map.* A mind map is a free-form outline that shows the connections between ideas and creates a visual image of a body of information.

▶ *Doing something new and different.* Take an art class or learn a musical instrument. Purposely pick up a magazine you wouldn't normally read and skim a few articles.

▶ *Breaking your routines.* Study in new places, talk to new people. Play a different kind of music in the background when you are trying to be creative.

► *Playing the five-senses game.* Try to think in terms of how you can use all your senses to make a project, subject or idea more interesting. If you are studying history, try to imagine how the Battle of Gettysburg would have smelled. What kind of food did the soldiers eat? What sounds did they hear as they fell asleep? What did the uniforms feel like?

► *Reading books or taking courses in creative thinking.* Take a look at *Creativity in Business* (Carol Kinsey Goman. Crisp Publications).

► *Storyboarding your ideas.* Storyboarding is a process that Disney studios originated for laying out animated movies. It also works for writing papers. First, formulate four or five basic questions that your report should answer. Write these questions on 4″ × 6″ index cards. Using 3″ × 5″ index cards, write only one idea, quote or definition that addresses the questions you have posed per card.

Stack the idea cards with the appropriate question cards. Do not worry about the order of the ideas right now, just write them down and place in the appropriate stack. If you find information that is interesting or relevant but does not answer one of your basic questions, copy it down on cards and start an ''other'' stack. When you have collected more than enough basic information for your report, spread out your cards so you can look at the big picture.

Now arrange the cards in the most logical order. Decide in what sequence the questions you have posed should be answered. Line these cards up at the top of your workspace. Now arrange the idea cards under the appropriate questions. Move the cards until you are satisfied with the order. Eliminate any that no longer seem important and add cards from the ''other'' stack if appropriate. When you have finished, all you will need to do is write the narrative that will hold your ideas and quotations together.

BE ADAPTABLE TO THE LEARNING SITUATION

To be a successful lifelong learner, you must be ready to adapt to different situations. These four common learning situations each require different behaviors and thinking styles from the learner.

1. The Traditional Classroom

The teacher talks, gives assignments and tests. The learner needs to be on time, read assignments, take notes and ask good questions. The traditional classroom frequently puts the learner in what looks like a passive role. But it is not enough merely to attend. To get the most out of the situation, the learner must be involved and well prepared to make sure that the material is mastered.

2. The Laboratory

The laboratory can be any situation where the learner gets the chance to practice with new information and skills. On-the-job learning is frequently done in a laboratory-type environment. The main ingredients for success in the laboratory situation are curiosity, sharp observation skills and the willingness to learn from mistakes. The learner needs to realize that experience is an excellent teacher, even if some of the experiences are failures.

3. The High-Tech Tutor

Computers, VCRs, video discs and audio books provide new ways to sharpen skills and expand knowledge. Each technology has its own advantages and challenges. The lifelong learner needs to overcome any reluctance or fear of technology to benefit from available options.

4. Independent Learning

People have always sought knowledge and skills on their own and have become self-taught masters. The key ingredients are a keen desire to continue growing and improving, the ability to set and reach goals without outside encouragement, understanding how to find necessary information, asking good questions and finding people who can act as mentors.

PART

3

Planning for
Lifelong Learning

PLANNING FOR LIFELONG LEARNING

Many people find that they are filled with good intentions about being a lifelong learner, but they never seem to get around to it. Interesting ideas and opportunities cross their path, but they always seem to be too late for registration, or they can't find the time to use the self-help cassettes they ordered. If learning is to be a priority, you must treat it like one. The following steps will help you get organized.

- *Set some learning goals.* Think about those things that you would like to know more about or be better at. Write your goals down. Define what you want to learn and by when.

- *Explore available resources.* Who teaches what you want to learn? What materials are in print? Are there opportunities for self-study? Many of these questions can be answered over the telephone or at the local library.

- *Include learning in your daily activities.* If you don't plan your day and create a list of things to do, now is a good time to start. Set aside 10 minutes in the morning or the evening before bed to think about what you would like to accomplish in the next day. Make a "to do" list that includes specific learning activities.

- *Decide when you will set aside time to learn on a regular basis.* Just like learning to play the piano or master your golf game, the secret is in consistent effort. Practicing 30 minutes a day, every day, is much more effective than cramming. Find time in your daily schedule for learning and self-improvement.

- *Take inventory of the materials and books that you already own.* Many of us are surrounded by unread books, cassettes we didn't listen to, half-started projects and tools that we never took time to learn to use. You don't always have to spend more money to get started on lifelong learning. Often the materials we need are already on hand.

- *Set your goals high enough to challenge, but not so high that they frustrate you.* Tasks that are either too easy or too hard tend to discourage learners. To stay motivated, strive for goals that are possible but not pushovers.

- *Check your progress along the way.* If your goal is to be fluent in Spanish in five years, set a short-term goal of being able to order dinner at a Mexican restaurant completely in Spanish by the end of the month. Set an intermediate-goal of being able to understand a Spanish language newscast by the end of the year. If you achieve your short-term goals, you will achieve your long-term goal.

LEARNING GOAL WORKSHEET

Select one short-term (one month), one medium-term (one month to a year) and one long-term (longer than one year) learning goal. Start the learning process by completing the form below.

Short-term learning goal:

Within the next 30 days, I will _____

_____

Resources to meet this goal are available from _____

I will set aside the following times to work toward this goal _____

_____

When I reach this goal, I will be able to _____

Medium-term learning goal:

Within the next year, I will _____

_____

Resources to meet this goal are available from _____

I will set aside the following times to work toward this goal _____

_____

When I reach this goal, I will be able to _____

Long-term learning goal:

Within the next _____, I will _____

_____

Resources to meet this goal are available from _____

I will set aside the following times to work toward this goal _____

_____

When I reach this goal, I will be able to _____

A TIME AND A PLACE TO LEARN

Many of the concentration problems that adults complain of when they try to learn are preventable. By paying attention to the time and place you have set aside for learning, you can create a personalized learning environment. Although where and when formal classroom learning takes place is often dictated to you, you can decide where and when to do your independent learning.

What Time Is Best for You?

Ask yourself these questions: What time of day am I the most alert? Am I an early riser who shines in the morning and goes downhill thereafter? Am I a night owl who just gets focused after the eleven o'clock news? Do I peak or crash in the midafternoon? Use this information to identify your best and worst times to study.

You may find that your "prime learning time" is outside your normal schedule. Many people who live and work in a busy environment find that very early in the morning before the rest of the house is awake or late at night after others have gone to bed offer the most distraction-free times. Just don't make the mistake of thinking that you can get by with less rest than you need—a tired brain loses much of its sharpness. Some adults try to postpone learning until "everything else is done"; the problem is, everything else is *never* done. Learning time must become a priority.

Where Is Your Prime Learning Location?

What you are trying to learn will affect where you choose to work. If you need particular tools, equipment or people, you may be restricted to a particular location.

If you need books only, consider these basics. First, your learning place should be used solely for that purpose. If at all possible, set up a spare bedroom, a corner of the basement or any other area that can be used exclusively as your study area. If this is not possible, at least move out of the normal traffic pattern in your home or go to the library. Ask yourself:

1. **Is the level of sound comfortable to you?** Silence is golden for some people, others need a little background noise. If you can't find a completely quiet place, consider using soft, instrumental music such as classical or light jazz to mask the noise in the environment.

2. **Do you have all the supplies that you will need?** Nothing is more irritating or disruptive than running out of supplies. A well-stocked study area should have pens, paper, tape, rulers, stapler, typing or computer supplies and basic reference books such as a good dictionary and thesaurus. As you focus your interests, you may want to start your own private library.

3. **Is it reasonably (but not too) comfortable?** You should be comfortable, but alert. Your furniture doesn't have to be fancy, but it should be inviting enough that you can focus. On the other hand, trying to read while lying down is asking for a nap. If sleepiness is a frequent problem for you, try studying standing up. Thomas Jefferson and Ernest Hemingway wrote that way.

4. **Is it fairly uncluttered?** A learning place should have some sense of order to it. Try to limit the material on your workspace to what you are using and develop a filing system for materials that you want to keep.

5. **Is the light good enough?** Experiment with several lamps and bulb strengths to get the right amount of light.

6. **Does it encourage you to work?** The atmosphere should be appealing and stimulating. There should be a sense that "this is a place I can focus."

If you answered "no" to any of the above questions, what can you do about it? Is your area "fixable," or do you have to find a new place of work? Sometimes a simple move from a busy part of the house to a quiet spot in the basement can make a great deal of difference. If no place in your home is adequate, consider carrying a special "learning briefcase" that includes all your supplies. You may find that your best study area is a library, an empty classroom on campus or even your office after work hours.

PART

4

Learning to Listen, Listening to Learn

LEARNING TO LISTEN, LISTENING TO LEARN

Listening is not an easy skill to learn or to teach. We often confuse listening with the natural and passive act of hearing. But productive listening is much more than just hearing, it is also understanding and acting on what is said.

It is often difficult to tell whether a listener really understands a message. It is not a directly observable skill like riding a bike or playing the guitar. With listening, we have to observe secondhand outcomes: How did we do on the test? Did we follow the instructions accurately? It is even possible to fool ourselves into believing we were listening when, in fact, we were merely hearing sounds without focusing on meaning.

Pay Attention to Your Attention

Every year dozens of articles are printed on the topic of listening that give very good advice that is nearly impossible to follow. The advice tells you to pay attention, avoid being distracted and focus on main ideas.

This advice is given to students, counselors and businesspeople all the time. What these people are being asked to do is pay attention to their attention, a skill that very few people, if any, have really mastered. Just concentrating can be a difficult business. Being aware of whether or not you are concentrating is even harder.

Why Can't I Just Concentrate?

Concentration is at the heart of listening. When we say that we haven't been listening, we are saying that we haven't been concentrating on what was said.

Concentration is hard to master because it usually comes about as a result of something interesting. It is often hard to start concentrating on a new topic unless it grabs our interest. Since something is always already going on in our heads, any new input must battle for our attention.

Try this experiment: Do not think of anything for just a moment. Tough, isn't it? Your brain seeks stimulation, and if nothing happens to stimulate it, you will find something to think about. Often, random thoughts, memories and wishes will race through your brain for no apparent reason. These thoughts often interfere with our ability to listen.

A DIFFERENT APPROACH

> *We are more likely to act ourselves into feeling,*
> *than we are to feel our way into acting.*
> —William James

The idea is this: maybe our internal states (inattention, depression) are the results of external behaviors, not the other way around. Instead of, "I was doodling in class because I was bored," maybe "I was bored because I was doodling!" Instead of, "I take lousy notes because I hate history," maybe "I hate history because I take lousy notes!" Instead of, "I didn't finish the report because I'm depressed," maybe "I am depressed because I didn't finish the report!"

This may not sound like a radical idea at first, but it does give us a fresh way to approach old problems: instead of thinking about concentrating, behave in a way that will help you concentrate, understand and remember what was said. By being prepared, acting interested and getting involved, your ability to concentrate will be greatly improved. Don't wait to be in the mood. Get started and act interested—often your enthusiasm will grow as a result of your actions.*

Productive Listening

Our daily lives are rich with passive learning experiences. Students attend lectures; employees attend meetings. Adults spend countless hours in situations where one or two people do the talking and the rest are supposed to soak it up. This idea contradicts what we know about the way people learn. We learn by being active users of new information, not passive hearers.

Productive listening starts by understanding ourselves and the listening situation. Listening is a complex act of moving information from one human brain to another by converting ideas into words in the speaker's mind and words back into ideas in the listener's mind. These words frequently have a variety of possible meanings and are strung together in a less-than-perfect fashion.

Before the listener understands the words, they must pass through many communication filters or distractions, that can alter or sometimes even block the original meaning of the message. Some distractions we are very aware of, like the noise in the room next door or the voice of the impolite whisperer two seats over. We may not be aware of others. The listening distraction inventory is designed to help you become aware of those things that tend to distract you the most.

*Horn, Sam. *Concentration: How to Focus for Success.* Crisp Publications.

LISTENING DISTRACTION INVENTORY

Rank order the following factors according to how much they interfere with your ability to listen effectively. Use the number 1 to indicate the factor that has the greatest negative impact on your ability to listen, a number 2 for the second greatest, and so on.

A. _____ Noise and activity in the immediate area

B. _____ A speaker with an unpleasant voice

C. _____ Profanity

D. _____ Ideas that are different from your own

E. _____ Dress or hairstyle that is different from your own

F. _____ Your own internal thoughts and concerns

G. _____ A large age difference between you and the speaker

H. _____ An accent that is different from your own

I. _____ A speaker who talks down to you

J. _____ A disorganized speaker

K. _____ Prior negative experience with the speaker

BATTLING OUR PERSONAL DISTRACTORS

By becoming aware of those things that distract us the most, we can better prepare to battle our own biases and weak spots. We set ourselves up for poor listening by focusing too much on how the message is delivered and not enough on the content. Below are tips for each of the distractions on the survey. Focus on your top five personal distractors.

A. **Noise and activity in the immediate area** — Do what you can to control distractions by taking a quiet seat and limiting your view of people and activity. If you cannot control the distraction, acknowledge that it exists and then focus on your listening, not the distraction. If you have trouble seeing or hearing what is going on in a class, get there early enough next time to pick a prime seat.

B. **A speaker with an unpleasant voice** — Listen for content, not style. Many very informative people have poor public speaking skills. The more you think about how much the professor sounds like Elmer Fudd, the less you will hear content.

C. **Profanity** — Some people think that the use of profanity makes their message more powerful. However, research has shown that some people so dislike swearing that they can't hear the message. Focus on content, not word choice; if you are truly offended, you may need to raise your concerns with the speaker.

D. **Ideas that are different from your own** — Learning is about being exposed to ideas. You do not have to change your mind in order to listen and understand another point of view. When you are exposed to very different ways of looking at the world, try comparing and contrasting your own ideas with the speaker's instead of resisting the new information. You will be better equipped to defend your point of view if you understand the other side.

E. **Dress or hairstyle different from your own** — Although society has become much more open about style, most of us still have our own expectations surrounding appearance. Be open. Many brilliant teachers have worn funny-looking clothes or parted their hair in a strange way.

F. **Your own internal thoughts and concerns** — Do everything you can to become actively involved in listening. If you still find that your mind is wandering, pull yourself back to the lecture. It may help to jot down your unrelated concerns so that you can free your mind up to focus on the task at hand. Don't get frustrated with your wandering mind; instead, gently refocus.

G. **An age difference between you and the speaker** — ''That young pup'' or ''that old fogey'' are both examples of age prejudice. People often place too much importance on age and not enough on knowledge. Knowledge can come from people of any age.

H. **An accent that is different from your own** — Many scholars from other countries teach in the United States. Try to relax. Accents can be more difficult to understand if you try too hard. Don't be afraid to ask when you do not understand something; most instructors want to make themselves understood and will be glad to help you. Form notetaking teams with other students to compare notes after class.

I. **A speaker who ''talks down to you''** — Most of the time, the slight is unintentional. People who have studied a topic for many years may use language that they think is basic when, in fact, students may not understand it. Be prepared: Read assignments and memorize new vocabulary before class. Ask questions when you don't understand, and form a notetaking team for your class.

J. **A disorganized speaker** — The best advice is to be prepared: Read assignments and memorize new vocabulary before class. Ask when you don't understand, and form a notetaking team for your class. Leave plenty of extra blank space in your notes for filling in ideas as the instructor skips around.

K. **Prior negative experience with the speaker** — It is possible for learners to have an unresolved conflict with an instructor. But unless you can choose another instructor, remember to focus on your goals for being in the class, not on who the instructor is. If you fail to learn, you are the one who loses.

CASE STUDY

Bill: A Case Study

Bill has been working on a college degree at night for the last two years.
When he gets to class at 7 p.m. he is already tired from a full day's
work. Bill's job as a manager is one that he has trouble leaving behind.
He is constantly thinking of the people and projects that are under his
direction. Just today, his boss told him he has to cut another five percent
from his already tight operating budget.

On the nights that he takes statistics class he barely has enough time to
stop home and grab something to eat before class. Tonight, as he rushed
in and out of the house, his two children were arguing, and his wife told
him that his son's teacher had sent a note home about a failing grade.
He grabbed his books and promised to "deal with it later." On the way
to the campus, Bill noticed his car made a grinding noise each time he
used the brakes.

After spending 10 minutes looking for a place to park, he rushed in three
minutes late and got the last seat, by the door near the noisy hallway.
He hadn't looked at his statistics homework since last class and he felt a
sinking feeling when the graduate student began explaining brand new
material. He strained to understand the terms through the accent of the
instructor and wondered whether a teacher that young could really have
known what she was talking about. As the problem was written on the
board he thought, "I hate math. I never was any good at this stuff."

The woman in front of him reminded him of an employee he had to lay
off last month and he thought of the budget. A voice in the hallway
sounded like his son and he thought of the failing grade. From nowhere,
the sound of the screeching brakes rang in his head and he wondered
how much the car repairs would cost.

Looking up at the board, he realized the instructor had erased the first
example and was explaining another. "Darn, I'll never understand this
stuff," he thought.

What advice would you give Bill?

Advice to Bill

If we assume that Bill made a good choice in pursuing his degree at this stage of his life, then we must accept the realities of his world and the challenge of this statistics class. If this is a required course for his major (it doesn't sound like he took it for fun), then Bill has a very clear goal: pass the class and leave with as much useful knowledge as possible. He certainly won't want to drop the class (a waste of time) or fail (a waste of time, money and ego). Bill needs to accept the need for the class and recognize how it fits into his goals.

Bill should not rush home for dinner; he should pack a meal that he can eat somewhere on campus. He should leave work at quitting time and head straight for campus. Parking is usually much easier between 4 p.m. and 6 p.m. after the day-student rush and before the evening-student rush. He should find a spot to eat and study that is quiet enough to review his notes from last week.

The first place to look for study space is the statistics classroom. If it is empty, Bill should take the best seat in the house, about three rows back and in the center of the room. This will put him directly in the instructor's line of sight and close enough to understand what is said. It will also get him away from that noisy hallway. The other students who sit in the front of the room will tend to be the ones most interested in the course. They will be good to get to know to review notes with or to form study groups.

Bill needs to put away everything except statistics and start by reviewing old material. He should write out any questions he has about the homework. Almost all math instructors start class by asking, ''Were there any questions about the homework?'' He should be ready. Then Bill should check the syllabus (course outline) to see what is to be covered tonight.

He should mentally become a student and put work, home and finances on the back burner. He cannot do anything about those issues while he sits in this classroom. If thoughts about work, home and car repairs persist, he should write them in a small pocket calendar to address tomorrow. Writing them down helps put them out of his mind for now by assuring him that he won't forget. Bill should try to be mentally where he is physically: in the classroom.

When class starts, it is important to relax and focus on the material, not the age, sex or accent of the instructor. If you relax and try, you will get better at understanding accented speech. If Bill can't understand, he must ask; chances are 10 other students have the same question. If he doesn't want to interrupt but wasn't clear on something, he can mark the note page with a question mark and later ask the instructor or a fellow student for help.

ADVICE TO BILL (continued)

Immediate review is best. After class, Bill should take at least five to 10 minutes to correct and complete his notes and try one problem from the homework. This 10 minutes can save hours later in the week.

Telling yourself how bad you are at math is a self-fulfilling prophesy. If Bill needs help, he can get a tutor. Almost all schools have tutor referrals; some will even pay the tutor. Many places have free ''help rooms.'' If Bill understood the prerequisite math courses, he should do all right in this one. If he didn't, he may have registered over his head. That is one case where dropping the course might be the best bet. You can't run before you can walk.

One more thing. Bill should thank his spouse for handling the kids while he is in class. He needs to take time to talk and listen to what is going on at home and not get caught in the trap of being the old grouch that lays down the law in his infrequent waking hours at home. His family's support will be very much needed if Bill is to reach his goal.

LISTENING AS A THREE-STAGE PROCESS

Aggressive listening can be very demanding. If we are listening in an important situation at work, in a class or at home, we should look at listening as a three-stage process:

1. Mental transition

2. Physical transition

3. Engagement

Each of these stages involves a series of simple steps, a kind of listening checklist. There is no way to devise an exact formula for every situation, but when you are listening to produce results of some kind, to make a sale, to pass a test, to complete a project, you should run through the checklist to ensure that you do the best possible job of listening. With effort and practice this new approach to productive listening will become automatic.

THE THREE STAGES OF LEARNING

STAGE 1: MAKING THE MENTAL TRANSITION (READY)

The first stage of effective listening should happen before the conversation or class starts. This stage prepares you mentally for what you will hear. By shifting your attention before the communication begins, you will be better prepared to focus on the message. Just remember to be mentally READY.

Review your last contact with the speaker

When possible, prepare for your role as listener by reviewing the last time you listened to that particular person. One of the best ways to get the most out of a class is to review the lecture notes from the last class. This will focus your mind and prepare you to follow the flow of today's lecture.

Eliminate controllable distractions

Select a seat away from noisy hallways and impolite people. Set yourself up to focus on the information at hand. Put away any papers or books that may compete for your attention. Sit where it is easy to see the instructor and hard to see anything that may distract you.

Anticipate, but don't prejudge

Try to think ahead of the speaker, but don't be surprised if the lecture goes in a different direction. Thinking ahead makes you an active participant in the lecture. Reading assignments carefully before a lecture also gives you a head start.

Determine your listening objectives

Know why you are listening. Go into the class, seminar or meeting with questions in mind that you hope will be answered. Keep in mind why you decided to attend. Even if this is a required class that holds little interest for you, remember how it will help you reach a long-term goal.

Yank yourself into the present

All too often, learners bring their bodies to a seminar, but their minds are back at work or at home or on vacation. Don't fool yourself. In order to learn, you must focus on the moment that you are in. Adult learners have busy lives and a lot on their minds, but it's a waste of time to worry about yesterday and miss what's going on now.

STAGE 2: MAKING THE PHYSICAL TRANSITION (SWAT)

Stage two shows you how to assume the correct listening posture. This is the simplest, and perhaps most effective part of the three-stage process.

The nonverbal messages that we send by physically preparing to listen almost always improve communication by indicating that we are really interested in what is said. In addition, this posture sends the message to your brain that you are there to listen and learn.

Sit up and lean slightly forward

This is an alert posture that helps inspire an alert mind. Leaning back or slouching down invites sleepiness and makes notetaking more difficult.

Watch the instructor and visual aids

Watch as well as listen. By keeping an eye on the instructor, you will pick up additional information from visual aids, body language, gestures and facial expressions.

Acknowledge what you hear by nods, facial expressions and asking questions

Communication is always a loop: how you listen affects how someone speaks. The positive feedback of an attentive audience improves the quality of a lecture. More importantly, these outward expressions of interest help convince your own mind to concentrate.

Take notes

Although sometimes it feels like taking notes is distracting, a written record of a seminar or lecture will last much longer than your memory will. Especially if you are going to be tested, well-organized notes are essential.*

*Lengefeld, Uelaine. *Study Skills Strategies.* Crisp Publications.

STAGE 3: DURING AND AFTER THE PROCESS (FAR)

Now you are mentally and physically ready. In stage three you learn how to listen actively. To listen actively, we must take measures to ensure that we follow the speaker's train of thought.

Focus

Concentrate on the content of the lecture, not the instructor's appearance, accent, tone of voice or personality. Many instructors are not skilled public speakers. Remember why you are in class: to gain and refine your skills and knowledge. Increase your involvement in the lecture by nodding when you understand, involving yourself in discussions and picturing yourself applying the content of the lecture. Imagine yourself in a one-to-one conversation with the instructor: use the same kind of focused attention you would when listening to your best friend.

Abbreviate

Don't worry about spelling, correct English or handwriting when you take notes. As long as you can read and understand your notes at a later time, they will serve the purpose. Leave plenty of white space between topics and at the end of lines. This blank space will come in handy later when you fill in details and complete your thoughts. Leave a blank column on the left side of the page for markers, symbols and important terms.

Revise

If you can, refine your notes within 20 minutes after class. Make this a routine that you strictly follow. This revising session helps to capture new information before you forget it.

P A R T

5

New Learning
Technology

NEW LEARNING TECHNOLOGY

Today's world is filled with gadgets that can enrich and expand when, where and how we learn. No longer is the learner limited to the printed page or the lecture hall. No longer is the library a place that specializes only in books. Audiotapes, videotapes, video discs and computers all bring the world of high technology to the act of learning. All these tools can help to access information. Each has its own special strengths and weaknesses.

Many schools, colleges and companies are investing heavily in high-tech learning equipment. Home computers, VCRs and audio tape recorders also make it possible to take advantage of these advances at home and even in your car. By becoming familiar and comfortable with these new learning tools, you can expand your learning options, increase the time you can devote to self-improvement and add valuable technology related skills.

This section will help you consider the advantages and disadvantages of a variety of high-tech learning tools and provide advice for getting the most out of each type of technology.

AUDIOTAPE

Advantages

✔ Great for auditory learners

✔ Helps fill dead commute time

✔ Can listen and move around

✔ An alternative to reading for those who don't like to read or have trouble reading

✔ With the instructor's permission, you can use a tape recorder to capture entire lectures and review as you commute or work around the house. (This is a very time-consuming way to review and should be used only when lectures are too difficult to take good comprehensive notes.)

Bookstores and libraries now have entire sections devoted to books on tape (audiotaped versions of printed materials either in full-length or condensed forms). Originally, taped books were created for people with visual impairments or reading difficulties. Gradually, another market developed for busy people who want to ''read'' as they commute, paint the bedroom, exercise or mow the grass.

Disadvantages of Audiotape

Taped books are clumsy. To repeat a section, you must rewind, find the spot you want and replay the tape. You can't underline a cassette. You can't glance back if you didn't understand or you missed something. You have no graphs, pictures or maps to fall back on. The spoken reading voice is much slower than most of us can read, and it's impossible to skim.

Getting the Most from Audiotape

To help overcome the natural limitations of listening to taped books, try the following:

► Stop the tape and repeat aloud important ideas and facts that you would like to remember.

► Make notes soon after your listening session.

► Listen to important or difficult-to-understand tapes more than once.

► If the tape comes with a printed workbook or study guide, use it! Preview the print before listening, and stop the tape when you need to look at a chart or answer questions.

► Make sure that your recorder has a counter so you can mark where important information will be found.

► Consider buying a variable speed tape player that allows you to speed up tapes to a more challenging pace.

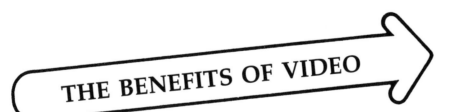
THE BENEFITS OF VIDEO

VIDEO AND VIDEOTAPE

Advantages

✔ Great for visual learners.

✔ A picture is worth a thousand words.

✔ Great for demonstrating physical skills.

✔ Easy to use at home.

✔ Tapes can be slowed down, reviewed.

✔ Tapes can pace instruction to an individual's speed.

✔ TV generation is comfortable with video.

✔ Available day or night for classes of one to 1,000.

✔ Tapes can be used as a feedback tool—for example, reviewing a tape with an expert of you performing a skill or seeing and hearing yourself give a speech.

Videotape has become a part of our everyday life. Most American families now own a VCR and many have their own video cameras. Video has largely replaced film in the classroom because it is easy to use and handle. Like movies, videos are great ways to see other places and other times. They also make it possible to watch experts or actors demonstrate the right way to put on a roof, solve a conflict, sell a car or repair a piece of equipment.

Libraries stock both entertainment and educational videos that can be borrowed or you can buy special tapes to have on hand to use whenever you like.

In the workplace, companies are investing heavily in video-based training because of the flexibility and relative cost-effectiveness of having experts on tape. Because it is feasible to have one student in the room at a time, video makes it possible to train only the people who need it when they need it.

Disadvantages of Videotape

People's biggest problem with video is that it looks and sounds too much like TV. Students frequently settle into a classic TV-viewing mode while using educational video: slack-jawed, bleary-eyed and passive, passive, passive. Using video means that you are tied to two pieces of large and expensive equipment, the VCR and the monitor. Furthermore, video is expensive to produce; production companies may try to recoup their investment by selling a watered-down product to the widest possible market. Companies that buy the video frequently use it long after it has become dated to maximize their investment. Lastly, like audiotape, it is difficult to skim or review isolated pieces of video; much time can be wasted rewinding and searching if a very comprehensive guide is not provided.

Getting the Most from Videotape:

► Be selective. The quality of video varies drastically. Don't waste time on the bad stuff.

► Treat video like any other class. Take notes, answer the questions that are asked and become actively involved.

► Look for videos with extensive print support in the form of workbooks, quizzes and study guides.

► Preview all printed material.

► Educational video only looks like commercial TV. Don't be fooled into a passive approach.

► Take frequent breaks if you are losing your concentration.

► If the video is part of a class, don't hesitate to ask the instructor for clarification. If you don't want to interrupt, write your questions down to ask at the end.

► Use the counter to note where important information is located on the tape.

VIDEODISC TECHNOLOGY

Advantages

Interactive video shares all the advantages of traditional videotape, plus:

✔ Videodiscs combine the power of video and the speed of computers.

✔ It is possible to store more information on a disc.

✔ It is possible to access information almost instantly from any place on the disc.

✔ Pictures are usually sharper using disc technology.

✔ Better systems and programs can branch, or go where the learner needs or wants to go instead of following one set, linear track like videotape.

Videodiscs, sometimes called laser discs, are large silver platters usually about the size of a record album that work very much like a compact disc (CD). A beam of light (laser) reads the information on the disc and produces pictures and sounds on a video monitor. The monitor is connected to a computer keyboard or has a touch screen that the student uses. The great advantage of disc technology over tape is that a disc need not run from beginning to end. The machine can find any information on the disc quickly either at the direction of the user or as a response to an answer. This ability is what makes video truly interactive.

Well-programmed discs can steer learners according to their interests and abilities. A math lesson will analyze the learner's mistakes and try to identify a common weakness, say, the inability to multiply fractions. The disc will then suggest, and sometimes insist, that a review of that skill should be completed before going further. Another example of this flexibility: A lesson may present a situation and ask the learner to choose from a preset list of possible actions. By choosing an option, the student is guided through one of several possible scenarios. This ability to choose from one of many preprogrammed options is known as branching. By following the learner's responses, the equipment can present material in a personalized order and at the appropriate speed. In this way, the disc can become a highly personalized tutor.

Disadvantages of Videodisc

Cost is probably the biggest drawback to videodisc technology. Well-designed materials are very expensive to create and program. The equipment to play the disc is also much more expensive than a standard VCR, and its quality varies greatly.

Another disadvantage for some students is the absence of human interaction. While it is possible to design a total learning experience that considers the need for human interaction, videodiscs are usually used by individuals in isolation. Finally, as with all instruction that is costly to program and produce, videodiscs frequently become dated long before they are replaced. As old-fashioned as a professor's lecture notes may seem, it is still much easier to update a lecture than any of these high-tech tools.

Getting the Most from Videodiscs

Becoming comfortable with the technology is the number-one factor in getting the most out of videodisc technology. Interactive videodisc technology is still a much less common tool than audio- and videotape. Look for the opportunity to work with this type of teaching aid and, when you find it, become oriented to its mechanics. Most of the better programs will then guide you through the process.

COMPUTER-ASSISTED INSTRUCTION (CAI)

Advantages

✔ Access to huge pools of information

✔ Paced to the learner's speed and ability

✔ Endlessly patient teacher

✔ No need to be embarrassed by what you don't know

✔ Learner can start class anytime of the day or night

✔ Good programs will not review what you already know or start over your head

✔ With the right equipment, you can learn at work, school or at home, when you want to learn

---

Computers have become important educational tools in and out of schools. Computer-assisted instruction is one of the fastest growing sectors of the lifelong learning movement, and programs are available to teach many subjects. Network services provide access to mountains of information, including electronic encyclopedias, stock quotes, research services and newspapers from around the world. For a monthly fee and a usage charge, anyone with a computer, a modem (a device for sending and receiving data over the phone) and a telephone can be hooked up to a giant pool of information.

Disadvantages of Computer-Assisted Instruction

Although prices have dropped dramatically, it still is much more expensive to buy a home computer and programs than it is to get a library card. Furthermore, the quality of CAI materials varies greatly. Some programs are not much more than electronic copies of printed workbooks. In addition, many adult learners fear computer technology, although most young people have grown up surrounded by computers and look on them with no more awe than the last generation did the telephone.

Getting the Most from Computer-Assisted Instruction

► Before investing in a computer and programs, try a few out—you may find that you do not need your own equipment.

► Treat the computer like any other electronic servant: turn it on, tell it what to do and turn it off when you're done.

► Ask the experts for advice on the best software and on-line services.

► Get comfortable with the machine in a light-hearted way: Play some computer games before diving into a challenging learning experience.

► Don't guess at answers. Most computer programs use a multiple-choice format, but the computer can't tell the difference between a guess and knowledge. If you guess correctly, you may be moved ahead too quickly. Make sure that you understand a concept before moving forward.

PART

6

Learning from Printed Materials—Reading

LEARNING FROM PRINTED MATERIALS

> *"Reading is a dynamic act, the creative coming together of minds."*
> —Waldo Frank

It's not fancy, but reading is still the most portable, versatile and flexible way to gather new information. While there are thousands of instructional videos on the market, there are millions of books, magazines and manuals. Being an effective reader is still one of the most powerful ways to be a lifelong learner.

Even though reading is universally taught in our society, it is not always mastered. Even proficient readers sometimes find themselves in the frustrating position of rereading material. Reading can become so automatic that even though we hear the individual words in our heads, the meaning eludes us.

The key to reading comprehension is to become mentally involved with the print in such a way that you always think about what you read. Reading is thought, guided by print. Most of the time when readers face a comprehension problem, they blame the book. They say it's too boring, hard or poorly written.

However, nothing can be done about the book. Writing is the author's job and, for better or worse, that job is done. Reading is the learner's job, and a skilled reader can often make up for a boring author.

The main causes of poor reading comprehension are passive reading style and poor concentration. To learn from printed material, your mind must be focused and your reading style must be aggressive. How well you remember what you read depends on the intensity of work you do on the information.

To read aggressively, you need a system. Try the following four-step approach to increase your comprehension.

THE FOUR-STEP PROCESS

Step 1: I Know

To focus your concentration and begin acquiring new information, you must first link what you already know about the topic with what you are about to read. Look over the title and read the first paragraph. Think over other material that has led up to this section. Write down a few things that you already know about the topic.

Step 2: I Predict

Anticipating or predicting what comes next will prepare your mind to receive new information. Think of predicting as posing a series of questions to yourself and reading as the act of looking for the answers.

Begin each session by previewing a section that you can read in about 20 minutes. During this preview, look over all bold-faced type, any charts, graphs or illustrations; pick a few sentences at random and read them. At the end of your preview, stop and write down a few predictions about what you are about to read. What are some questions you should be able to answer by the end of this section?

Step 3: Read Aggressively

Read with a pen in your hand. Underline, make notes, write in the margins. If you cannot write in the book, make notes that will refer you to particular pages in the book. Use symbols and diagrams to emphasize information that you need to remember. If you are preparing for a test, mark those passages that look like logical choices for test questions.

Step 4: Review and Summarize

At the end of each 20-minute reading block, review what you have read. Test yourself to see what you have retained. Without looking at the book, summarize the material. Start the summary with the words, ''I learned.'' For example, ''I learned that the start-up sequence for operating the Supercomplex Robotic Widget Maker is . . . .'' Stopping to summarize helps comprehension and memory.

Activity: Learner-Centered Reading

Use this page to practice learner-centered reading. Pick out a selection of reading material that you can read in about 20 minutes and follow the steps below.

1. Look at the title and first paragraph and then write a summary of what you already know about this topic. Tie the information to previous readings or classes.

   I know _____

   _____

   _____

   _____

   _____

2. Look over the selection and read all bold type, diagrams or illustrations and then predict what you are about to learn. Pose at least four questions to yourself.

   I predict _____

   _____

   _____

   _____

3. Read, and make sure your thoughts are guided by what you read. Underline, make notes and use symbols as you read. If you cannot mark in the book, make a simple outline of the content.

4. When you have finished reading, write down what you have learned without looking back at the selection.

   I learned _____

   _____

   _____

   _____

IMPROVING YOUR CONCENTRATION

Reading, like most tasks, requires concentration. To improve your ability to concentrate, eliminate as many distractions as possible. Make sure that you are getting adequate rest, a good diet, and enough exercise. Finally, concentrate in short bursts. Most people can concentrate for 15–20 minutes at a time. These short bursts of study time are much more effective than four-hour cram sessions.

You may want to buy a timer to prevent clock watching and help you create an achievable goal. To start off, set the time for five or 10 minutes. At the end of the time, take a short break—about one minute of break for every five minutes of concentration.

Build up until you can concentrate for 20–25 minutes and earn a five-minute break. At the end of the break, begin the process again. At the end of the third 20-minute session, you may want to reward yourself with a longer break or a treat of some kind.

Finish each concentration session by reviewing what you have learned. Jot down a short summary and review important details, including charts, headings and your own notes and markings.

You may not want to work, but force yourself to pretend to concentrate. Move to your study area, preview the material, set your timer and act like you are concentrating. Sometimes all you need is the willpower to start. Once the brain is engaged, real concentration will take over. If you wait to be in the mood, you may never start.

7

Making the Most of Your Memory

MAKING THE MOST OF YOUR MEMORY

Many myths surround human memory capacity. Memory is not like a box that fills up; in fact, the more the brain is used, the more ''connections'' we make in the brain. The more connections we make, the easier it is to find and use information, in other words, to think. Our brain is like a Tinker Toy structure: the more we add to the structure, the more potential connections we create, and we add to this memory network throughout our entire lives.

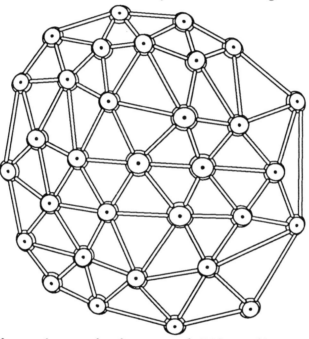

Mnemonics: Association and Visualization

Mnemonics are techniques for improving memory. They were probably used before written language to help recall complicated hunting and trading routes or retell the history of a tribe. Mnemonics are formed with visual images, rhythm or rhyme, association or connections to previously learned material. Some examples of mnemonics devices are:

- i before e except after c (spelling rule using rhythm and rhyme)

- Every good boy does fine (music rule using connections)

- H. O. M. E. S. (geographical rule for remembering the Great Lakes—**H**uron, **O**ntario, **M**ichigan, **E**rie, **S**uperior—association and acronym)

- **M**any **v**ery **e**arly **m**aps **j**ust **s**how **us** **n**ine **p**lanets (geographical rule to remember planets in order from the sun—**M**ercury, **V**enus, **E**arth, **M**ars, **J**upiter, **S**aturn, **U**ranus, **N**eptune, **P**luto—using connections)

MIND MAPPING FOR MEMORY

Mind mapping is a creative way to organize information. Mind maps are used for planning, organizing, studying and notetaking. They also work well as memory-assisting devices. They work well for most people because they simulate the way the brain is organized. Connections are created between bits of information and organized around a central theme. Each connection can lead the learner back to the central theme or on to another connection. This is what a simple mind map about memory might look like:

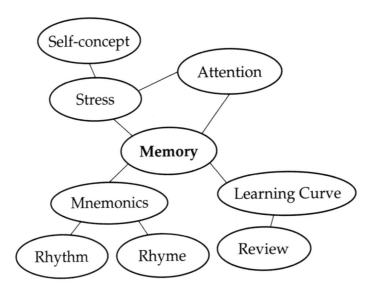

Here are some additional memory basics:

- Make sure you hear, see, feel, touch or taste it correctly. If it doesn't impress your senses or you get it wrong at first, you cannot possibly retrieve it correctly.

- Pay attention. You remember what you focus on. Much of what happens around you is lost simply because you did not pay attention.

- Review (think about, picture, write or say) the new information within 15 seconds. Mentally repeating what you want to remember signals the brain that this information is worth capturing. The more ways you review, the more likely you are to remember.

- Organize the information to remember it longer.

- Use your imagination and have fun. The mind best remembers imaginative, interesting, ridiculous, colorful images. If you can make vivid associations with boring information, the image will become your retrieval device.

- Relax. It is harder to learn when you are nervous.

THE NAME GAME

One very common and frustrating learning task is mastering new names. "I'm terrible at remembering names," people say, "but I never forget a face." Remembering names is difficult for several reasons:

- We are often distracted by external noise while we are being introduced.

- We are often distracted by internal noise; we're so busy thinking about what we will say next that we don't pay attention to the person's name.

- Our memory is overloaded by having so many new names to remember at once.

- Names are often just meaningless sounds—names like Bob, Sue and Frank have little meaning at first glance.

- We live up to our own self-fulfilling prophesy of being terrible at remembering names.

When you meet someone new, try the name game. To do this, create a meaning for the new name. As you are introduced, think of a phrase or word that sounds like the name you are learning. Here's how it works:

1. Listen carefully to the name to find meaning. If you think a moment, Bob does mean to be bounce up and down, Sue is what happens in court, and Frank means to be direct and honest. With a name like Alice, which does not have an obvious meaning, play "sounds like"; for example, Alice sounds like A-List.

2. Create an image of an object or action that the name sounds like.

3. Repeat the name as soon as possible and again at the end of the conversation.

4. Concentrate on the details of the person's face.

BEAT THE FORGETTING CURVE

Even when we try to remember new information, we will forget. Forgetting is a natural, predictable process, which begins as soon as learning takes place. New information is lost rapidly, especially in the first 20 minutes after learning. Seventy to 90% of new information can be lost in a single day.

- If you want to remember something, review it within 20 minutes.

- Break long study sessions into 20-minute blocks followed by 5-minute reviews.

- Use a spaced-practice schedule. Twenty minutes a day for five days is much better than two hours at one sitting.

- Make it meaningful.

- Organize information into chunks of seven items or less, which suits most people's short-term memory capabilities. If you must memorize a long list of 25 items, divide it into four smaller lists grouped in some logical fashion.

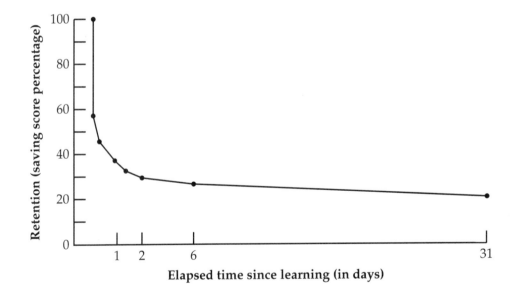

Your Powerful Visual Memory

Visual memory is usually more powerful than your memory for words or numbers or sounds. Unfortunately, much of what you are expected to memorize is hard to visualize. Facts, numbers and names do not provide easy-to-remember images like faces, scenery and pictures do. When it is not possible to turn the information into real pictures, creative mental images can help do the same thing.

PROCESSING NEW INFORMATION

Studying should be more than just reading. And learning should be more interesting than endless repetition of information. When studying, switch modes of thinking and interacting with the new material. Don't just read it—say it, listen to it, write it and make up mental images of it. The more ways you can process it, the better. For example:

- Visualize it—see it in full color, see it working.

- Say it into a tape recorder and play it back as you commute.

- Draw a diagram of it.

- Sing it.

- Debate it with a friend.

- Make up an acronym or a stimulus sentence.

- Rhyme it.

- Relate it to a past experience.

- Imagine how you might use it in the future.

- Make flashcards.

- Organize it in several different ways.

- Make up a story using key elements of the information.

- Outline it.

- Write in the book.

- Use a highlighter.

- Make a mind map connecting related ideas.

MEMORY AND AGING

Some changes come with aging. The good news for lifelong learners is that loss of memory is not necessarily one of them. The changes aging brings may affect your ability to learn indirectly, however. By being aware of these changes, it is possible to compensate for them.

Weakening of Sight, Hearing and the Other Senses

The sharpness of the eyes and ears usually declines with age. If new information does not make a clear impression on the sensory organs, it is not the fault of memory when the information is not recalled correctly. Frequent sight and hearing tests will keep these changes from sneaking up on you. Hearing and vision can often be corrected with glasses and hearing aids or simply by carefully choosing where you sit in a class or meeting and asking people to speak louder if you cannot hear.

General Health

The condition of the mind is related to the condition of the body. Exercise, rest and good nutrition are important to maintain high-functioning memory and thinking skills. One of the best ways to stay sharp mentally is to stay sharp physically.

Speed of Recall

Reaction time slows with aging, including the time it takes to recall information—but the decline is a very slow, gradual one. The recall time of a 50-year-old is about the same as a 15-year-old. After 50, it may take a little longer to respond to questions. But whatever adults lose in speed is generally made up for in accuracy and quantity of knowledge.

Retention

If what they learn is meaningful and interesting, older people retain it about as well as anyone. The problem is, the longer we live, the more we have seen, and sometimes the "new" fails to impress us. Snowfall doesn't have the magic it did when we were twelve; our fiftieth trip to the lake isn't as exciting as our first. We don't pay as much attention, especially if we know we will not use the information soon. To keep learning, surround yourself with new and interesting activities and people. Search for personal meaning and application in the new information that you encounter.

Distraction

Background noise, other conversations and other activity in the room tend to become more distracting as we age. The change begins as early as 30 and becomes more evident as we get older. A clean, quiet, organized workplace is an asset at any age, but may become a necessity as we get older.

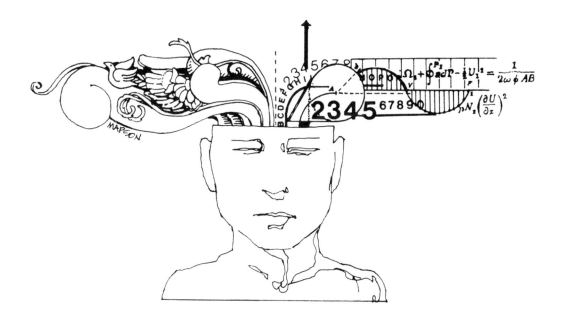

EXTERNAL MEMORY AIDS

Memory techniques are not meant to replace the use of external memory aids—that is, tools that are created to help us remember. Calendars, files, lists and electronic reminders can remove much of the burden from our memories and the chance from our daily lives.

Calendars

A calendar should both tell you about today and warn you about upcoming events for which you need to prepare. A reminder on April 15 that taxes are due may be too little too late. To be effective, the tax reminder should appear on March 15 with the note: taxes due one month, get to work.

Lists

Creating lists and following through on them is one of the most efficient aids to memory and time management. Set aside time to create a daily list and then refer to it several times throughout the day to stay on track and add new items. The feeling of accomplishment that comes from checking off completed tasks can act as a built-in reward system.

Pick-Up Points

It is very frustrating to get to the office and realize that the report you should be working on is at home on the dining room table. Get in the habit of creating a pick-up point at home and at work. Put what you need at the pick-up point as soon as you think of it. The thought may not come again. Possible pick up points: on the table by the door, on a mantle or on top of a file cabinet. Always check your pick-up point before leaving.

Do Something Different (Ticklers)

When it occurs to you that you must remember to stop on the way home and buy a birthday card or take that vitamin you forgot this morning, do something different right when the thought occurs. Put your ring on the other hand, put your watch on upside down, put a paper clip on your key ring. Every time you notice "that something different," it will tickle your memory and should remind you of what you need to do.

Time Savers

Consistent habits save time. You never spend time looking for your keys if you always put them in the same place. You don't hunt for phone messages if you have one bound booklet where you write down all your messages. If a file folder is refiled correctly after each use, it is there when you need it. Habits are hard to change, but it is worth the effort to become a better-organized person.

Take Notes

When in doubt, write it down. Then you can give your full attention to what is at hand.

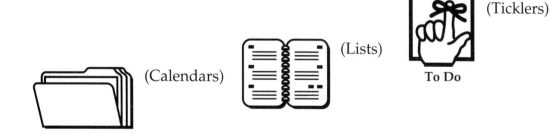

(Calendars) (Lists) (Ticklers) To Do

TIME MANAGEMENT AND MEMORY

Don't blame your memory for problems that are really caused by poor time management. Hurrying causes you to forget things you would ordinarily remember. Here are some tips to manage your time:

► Build both a planning time and a wrap-up time into your daily schedule. A few quiet moments to think ahead in the morning and a few moments at the end of the day before leaving work will do wonders to ensure that important details are not overlooked.

► Live in the present. Planning for the future is important, but being preoccupied with the past or the future will lead to missing out on what is going on now.

► Allow transition time between activities. Put things where they belong, write a date on your calendar and think over new information. Rushing from task to task can cause errors.

► Arrive ahead of time for appointments and meetings. The stress of being late can interfere with your ability to remember. Spend the extra time preparing for the meeting. Avoid overscheduling, which makes it impossible to be on time.

► Build time into your life for physical activity and fun.

Key Ingredients in Memory

Planning	Set memory goals
Interest	Natural or created
Focused Attention	Concentrate
Preview	Look ahead
Understanding	Look for meaning
Organization	Reorganize if necessary
Limitations	Make small groups of like items
Relate	What you know to what you are learning
Picture	See the information at work
Mnemonics	Use memory gimmicks
Practice	And practice and practice
Variety	Learn it a different way
Application	Use it soon

P A R T

8

Lifelong Learning
Options

LIFELONG LEARNING OPTIONS

Many educational options are available to you as a lifelong learner. Some of the more usual programs are described below.

Adult Basic Education

Programs designed to help adults master basic literacy and mathematics skills. Often offered through the public school system. May lead to earning a general equivalency diploma (GED), the equivalent of a high school diploma earned by passing a series of tests.

Independent Study

Learning on your own with no formal school, instructor or program. Can be done through books, tapes, video, hobbies, friends, travel, observation, jobs, etc. The most flexible, least structured path to lifelong learning, but offers no credentials to verify accomplishments. Many colleges and universities now offer programs that give credit for prior independent learning. Keep records of your independent self-study in the event you want the credentials.

Seminars

Offered through colleges, high schools, community centers or companies. Many are conducted at work on company time. They range in length from a few hours to several days (or longer). Many are offered in public locations like hotels or conference centers. Most offer informal proof of completion such as a certificate, some have been approved for continuing education units (CEUs). Be sure to keep records of your seminar attendance for possible portfolio credit or to be included in your personnel file.

Correspondence Study

Correspondence study is individual instruction by mail. Students can enroll any time, study at home, and set their own pace. Work is typically guided on a one-to-one basis with a faculty expert who designs materials, guides the student and grades or otherwise responds to student work. Both noncredit and credit programs are offered through correspondence. Credit can be earned at any level from elementary school through graduate programs.

LIFELONG LEARNING OPTIONS (continued)

Adult School

Programs range from diploma completion classes to hobby courses. Some classes are designed to teach job-related skills that will help students find specific types of employment.

Certificate Program

Generally one or more technical courses usually completed in one to 26 weeks. Normally the program focuses on one particular skill. Graduates receive a certificate verifying completion.

Diploma Program

A program offering technical and basic coursework. The program generally requires 600–1,500 hours or 40–90 quarter credit hours. Graduates receive a diploma upon completion.

Associate Degree

Community and junior colleges offer an Associate Degree or two-year degree, which refers to the length to the length of time most programs would take a student to complete if going to school full time. Programs include technical, basic and general courses.

Bachelor Degree

The basic degree offered by four-year colleges and universities consists of technical, basic and general courses.

Graduate Programs

Programs begun after completion of a bachelor degree that lead to a master, specialist or doctorate degree.

Gloria: A Case Study

Gloria's life is a very busy one. A single mother of two young children, she works full-time at a local hospital as a practical nurse, manages the household and spends as much time with her children as possible. She also lives in the same city as her aging parents and tries to help them out when they need her. She is living on a very modest income and knows that she and the children will need a larger paycheck as years go by.

She has begun thinking about getting a better job. She knows that the registered nurses she works with make much better money than she does and do some of the same work. She has talked to several of them about their education and has found that most of the new nurses have a bachelor's degree from a local university. She has had one brief conversation with an adviser from the university and was shocked at how long it would take to finish the bachelor's degree in nursing. She has also talked to the other nurses about the difficulty of the program, and they advised her that there were many, many hours of study involved. Since it has been 10 years since she last was in school, she doubts her ability to keep up.

Her goal of earning a better paycheck by becoming a registered nurse seems almost impossible with the demands of family and job. She is very discouraged.

CASE STUDY (continued)

Advice to Gloria

Gloria's situation is not unique. For many people, lifelong learning is not a luxury, but a matter of economic survival. Gloria needs to think and plan very carefully to ensure that she makes good decisions about her lifelong learning goals.

Gloria needs to explore her options more carefully. She is thinking about becoming a registered nurse because she needs a better paycheck. Is that the best way for her to get higher earnings? Beginning with her employer, she should talk to supervisors, the personnel office and other employees about options that could help her earn more money. She should also contact other employers to understand their needs and the opportunities outside the hospital. She should create as long a list as possible of her options. They may include job changes, overtime, learning a specialized skill that will make her more valuable, working premium replacement hours (weekends and evenings when others don't want to work) or going to school to prepare for a job change. For help with this exploration process, Gloria may want to take a career exploration course through a local community college or other source.

Gloria may find that she can be trained for another skilled position that will help her earn a better paycheck and require less preparation time than becoming an RN. If she does decide that becoming a registered nurse is the best option for her, she should now explore as many different ways to reach that goal as possible. Is a bachelor's degree really required? Will it bring the highest pay? Do hospitals in the area hire nurses from associate degree programs? From diploma programs? Are there any special programs to help practical nurses become registered nurses more quickly? What school is the most flexible in scheduling classes?

Only after this exploration stage is completed should Gloria decide what direction to take. If she decides to go back to school, the planning process is not over. She must consider child care, when and where she will study and how she will finance her education. The more planning she does, the less chance she has of frustration, discouragement and dropping out. Many special programs and services are offered at the local level to help adults in situations like Gloria's, and she needs to find out about them.

Gloria's road won't be easy, but if she doesn't start on it, she could find herself in the same situation five years from now.

LEARNING ON THE JOB

Opportunities to learn at work are growing dramatically. Nearly every organization is encouraging, even demanding that employees continue to expand their knowledge and skills. Unfortunately, many people see this as a threat. Instead, use this as an opportunity:

- Look at learning opportunities as a win-win situation. Your employer gets a better educated, more flexible employee and you gain more marketable skills. Your employer becomes more efficient and, presumably, more stable. You become a more valuable employee with a more stable firm and the greater personal freedom of increasing your options in the job market.

- Find out about your employer's formal educational policies and take advantage of them. Your company may pay for all or part of the cost of taking classes.

- Let your supervisor know that you are interested in upgrading your skills at work. Ask to be trained on new equipment or to learn new job functions. If you are interested in greater responsibility, become more flexible by mastering new skills.

- Find a mentor. Look around for someone who has skills and knowledge that you would like to gain. Tell that person that you are interested in learning what they know. Ask for advice, direction and help.

- Ask questions. Keeping secrets or covering up ignorance usually will cause you more problems in the long run. If you think that there may be negative consequences to telling your supervisor about a skill deficit, seek help at a community college, university or vocational school.

- Enroll in seminars and classes offered through the workplace. Knowledge is power, and it can mean security.

84

> ## Joseph: A Case Study
>
> Joseph has worked in the same medium-sized manufacturing plant for 21 years. He has been a supervisor for the last 10 years. Until recently, he had complete decision-making power for ordering supplies, scheduling work and assigning overtime. Recently, the company hired two young computer wizards to select computers and design programs to help make some of those decisions. They frequently use computer jargon in conversation that sounds like a foreign language to Joseph.
>
> Joseph feels as though he is losing some of his authority, and he is intimidated by the computers. He has never had the opportunity to learn about computer-assisted manufacturing and is afraid of looking stupid in front of the new employees. He is so uncomfortable with the changes around him that he is considering looking for a different job.

Advice to Joseph

Whether Joseph realizes it or not, the new computer programs are intended to help him and make his job easier, not intimidate him. First, he should ask his supervisors to be included in the planning stages, because the information for the programs should come from the people who use it every day. Joseph should request that he meet regularly with the programmers so that all relevant information is included.

At the meetings, Joseph should ask how the employees are to be trained on the equipment, how the equipment works, and what the goals are for its use. Joseph is probably not the only person threatened by the technology. He can ask to be trained first and can then help set up training for others.

As Joseph talks to the programmers, he should ask when he doesn't understand their jargon. He probably doesn't need to take an outside class, because the equipment and program at his job will be industry- and job-specific, but if he develops an interest in how computers work generally, this may be useful.

Final Activity

Your Case Study:
The First Entry in Your Learning Journal

Now it is time for you to start your lifelong learner's journal. You can use a notebook, journal, or personal computer. Keep records of your thoughts, ideas and accomplishments as a lifelong learner.

At the beginning of your journal, write a short case study like those you have read in this book. Include a description of your situation, goals, skills, attitudes and possible obstacles that you face. When you have finished, put your case study aside for a week. At the end of a week read it again and then write out your advice to yourself. Base your advice on the material in this book and your own thinking. This activity will serve both as a review of what you have learned and an opportunity for reflection. Good luck and good learning.

RELATED READINGS

Rose, Colin. *Accelerated Learning.*

Ellis, David. *Becoming a Master Student.*

Horn, Sam. *Concentration.* Crisp Publications.

Edwards, Betty. *Drawing on the Right Side of the Brain.*

Keith, Jon. *Executive Memory Techniques.*

Gardner, Howard. *Frames of Mind.*

Pauk, Walter. *How to Study in College.*

Loftus, Elizabeth. *Memory.*

Burley-Allen, Madelyn. *Memory Skills in Business.*

Wujec, Tom. *Pumping Ions.*

Bragstad, Bernice Jensen and Shrayn Mueller Stumpf. *Study Skills and Motivation.*

Lengefeld, Uelaine. *Study Skills and Strategies.* Crisp Publications.

Lorayne, Harry and Jerry Lucas. *The Memory Book.*

Gross, Ronald. *Peak Learning.*

Timm, Paul R. *Successful Self-Management.* Crisp Publications.

Lewis, David and James Greene. *Thinking Better.*

Bowles, Richard. *Three Boxes of Life.*

Herald, Mort. *You Can Have a Near Perfect Memory.*

Wonder, Jacquelyn. *Whole-Brain Thinking.*

NOTES

NOTES

NOTES

NOTES

NOTES

NOTES

NOTES

NOTES

OVER 150 BOOKS AND 35 VIDEOS AVAILABLE IN THE 50-MINUTE SERIES

We hope you enjoyed this book. If so, we have good news for you. This title is part of the best-selling *50-MINUTE*™ *Series* of books. All *Series* books are similar in size and identical in price. Many are supported with training videos.

To order *50-MINUTE* Books and Videos or request a free catalog, contact your local distributor or Crisp Publications, Inc., 1200 Hamilton Court, Menlo Park, CA 94025. Our toll-free number is (800) 442-7477.

50-Minute Series Books and Videos Subject Areas . . .

Management
Training
Human Resources
Customer Service and Sales Training
Communications
Small Business and Financial Planning
Creativity
Personal Development
Wellness
Adult Literacy and Learning
Career, Retirement and Life Planning

Other titles available from Crisp Publications in these categories

Crisp Computer Series
The Crisp Small Business & Entrepreneurship Series
Quick Read Series
Management
Personal Development
Retirement Planning